DESIGNS FROM

THE INTERIOR

DESIGNS FROM THE INTERIOR

POEMS BY

JOHN BARTON

(signature)

Anansi

First published in 1994 by
House of Anansi Press Limited
1800 Steeles Avenue West
Concord, Ontario
L4K 2P3
(416) 445-3333

Canadian Cataloguing in Publication Data
Barton, John, 1957-
Designs from the interior

Poems. ISBN 0-88784-558-4

I. Title.

PS8553.A78D47 1994   C811'.54   C94-930862-5
PR9199.3.B37D47 1994

Editing: Anne Szumigalski
Cover concept: Angel Guerra
Cover design: Brant Cowie / ArtPlus Limited
Cover photograph: David Young
Author photograph: Bev Chappell

Printed and bound in Canada

*House of Anansi Press gratefully acknowledges the support of
the Canada Council, Ontario Ministry of Culture, Tourism, and Recreation,
Ontario Arts Council, and Ontario Publishing Centre in the development
of writing and publishing in Canada.*

for Pam and Sue

because desires do not split themselves up, there is one desire touching the many things, and it is continuous.

Robert Hass

Contents

I   The Suburbs: Delivery   1

City in the Foothills   *3*
13047 Sherbrooke Avenue   *5*
The Hills   *7*
Delivery   *10*
Vocabulary   *12*
Setting   *15*
Nails   *17*
Who Is This   *19*
Pre-Architecture   *20*
Indian Graveyard, Gulf of Georgia, 1968   *24*
Physical   *25*
Stickmen   *27*
Notation   *31*
This Side of the Border   *36*

II   The City: Patriarchy   39

166B   *41*
Interior Design   *43*
After the Movies with O.   *46*
Parallel Lanes   *48*
Lives of the Saints   *50*
Ripper   *55*
For the Boy with the Eyes of the Virgin   *58*
Impotence   *61*
Physical Education   *64*
Best Man   *69*
For Magie at the Bedside of Her Dying Friend   *72*
The Aqua-Nuns   *74*
Artificial Intelligence   *76*
Patriarchy   *78*
Touch   *82*
Vernix   *83*

III   The Hinterland: Ecology   93

Mnemonics *95*
Noise *97*
Field Guide *99*
C-Level Cirque *101*
Ecology *103*
The Man from Grande Prairie *105*
West Then East *107*
Acadia Notebook *109*
Lift *113*
Time Pieces *115*
Stains *120*
Meech Lake, Late Afternoon *122*
Continuity *124*
Road, River, Snake *126*
California Notebook *128*

Acknowledgements 135

I The Suburbs: Delivery

Children may believe that they alone have interior lives.

Annie Dillard

City in the Foothills

What grows into my body
is night,
       the ink prairie sky above the dull
sodium glow of the street lamps as I
walk home
along the road I used to take
to and from school, sun setting
early or rising late in this cool country;
the houses snaking down the hill
on either side as I walk
familiar as the cold door keys clutched,
pulled from my coat pocket.

On this road my body altered
without me noticing.
My shoulders sloped forward;
my stride lengthened from the walk
back and forth, back and forth,
tuna sandwiches my mother made
squashed by books
with broken spines in my backpack.
Back and forth, home
through this spreading suburb,
arms swinging, eyes wandering
under the wings of a chinook.

In the distance the hills
are fallen horses, dusky brown in late winter,
their coats purple-brushed
each spring by the first crocus.
They will never rise from the sleep
they fell into when I was six,
the first day of school.

Let them dream,
for they have worked hard
pulling the carts that stood the weight
of provisions uncrated
before the mountains as this city grew:
the mahogany table and chairs,
photo albums, and maps I unfolded
with my sisters, with my mother and father.

13047 Sherbrooke Avenue

Something is singing
inside the cloth-covered box
left by my window
last night while I was sleeping.
Curtains that never quite meet
let in puzzle-pieces of sky
that God peers down from
and into my bedroom,
so blue and tidy,
my toys sound asleep
where I left them
curled up in a butter crate.

I am a good boy
and now something is singing.
I open my eyes to it,
to cloth draped over a box
filling with sunshine,
each leaf golden in its design.
A shadow moves through
its screen of green branches
and blood-red poppies.
It sings, hops
it seems, from one
foot to the next,
from one branch to one higher.
It pauses,
clattering something
like seeds down over something
that rattles like paper.

Behind the bars of my rib cage
something is singing.
It races,
fills my ears with its beating.
I am not yet old enough
to confuse *want* with *when*,
when with *waiting*.
I go to bed each night;
in the morning I wake,
tuned to the sounds of the family
I was born to and have
no thought of leaving,
my house opening
like a gift onto the street
where I play.

I lie in bed,
warm under the weight
of the blankets.
Laughter stirs through
the vents around me
and in the kitchen,
a radio blaring,
perhaps announcing that today
is my birthday,
that something is singing.

What pulls my new
four-year-old self
out of bed, makes me forget
to kick into my slippers,
footfalls cold against hardwood?
The leaf-patterned cloth
torn away —
a flash of yellow
and my wide eyes widening.

The Hills

Granny stands in a kitchen
that is not her own,
cigarette in one hand,
egg flipper in the other.
Hills caught in the window
above the sink are overcast,
mangy with winterkill.
Back turned away from them,
she takes down plates,
ashen face swimming up
at her as she lays the table.

Upstairs, the big
knock-kneed desk
she brought from her house
is filled with photographs
seldom shown or looked at.
Toward and away, the shiny
lid of the desk folds
down into the sun,
mahogany dented with the heaviness
of a hand hurriedly writing.
Sometimes I catch my face in it,
eyes like knots
snagged in the grain.

She used to tell stories.
The ones I remember
I still repeat to myself.
A young girl wrapped in furs
skates with her father
on a lake wide as the ocean,
the way across to the islands
ploughed and windy,
the stone city glinting
like ice in the corner
of her eye.

Sometimes the little girl
is smaller than me,
laid out on the pantry table,
and dizzy with something
sweet rising from the damp handkerchief
the doctor holds over her nose.
Slowly she counts backwards.

Toward and away, backwards
her stories lead me
only so far.
I tiptoe into her room.
Lavender bleeds
from closed dresser drawers.
I linger before a picture
of a man who died
before I was born.
No one's told me why
the medals that hang from
one corner of the silver frame
are pinned to his chest.

Across the hall in a bedroom
once my sister's,
now my own, toes pushing
against the bed's hard mattress,
knees locking, I crane
up toward the window.
Eyes at last
flush with the sill,
I stare across to
my best friend's house —
a thin girl with a budgie;
we love to skip rope.
Her house is red and peeling;
no one's at home.

Granny calls from the kitchen.
Often at lunch we are alone.
The grilled cheese sandwiches she's made
are salty islands swimming in fat
on the blue plates.
In silence we eat this
food that feeds the body only.
In silence the hills
shadow us, rain-soaked flanks
scored by fences and telephone poles,
the muddy streets like streams
running backwards
up the ravines.

Delivery

He is approaching.
The horse lumbers before the milk wagon,
one shod hoof before the other,
the gravel in the alley
grinding like teeth
as he dawdles between
stopping, waiting, and starting.

The milkman always catches up.
In his metal carrier
the neighbours' empties gleam,
secrets they trade
for cheese, whole milk,
and cool oblongs of butter.
The bottles blur as the man
leaps into the hold,
dark as any cupboard
or hiding place I have known.
Suddenly he jumps down
into the heat of late morning.
The wagon rocks,
urging the horse forward,
joints cracking as he shambles,
stops a few houses closer.

A few houses away
I wait outside the back gate.
Slats of white
flash as it swings,
creaking behind me.
The breeze teases
the cowlick I wetted down
quickly after brushing my teeth.
Next to my heart I hold
a shiny quart bottle scrubbed
clean by my mother,
embossed with my handprints.

Restrained by the fence,
I stand in the crabgrass,
a knee-high jungle loud with bees.
Around my left ankle
my mother knotted a hankie
to take away yesterday's sting.
I loosen the knot
and peek.
The sting turns into
heat-dazed butterflies
weaving across the cloudless
blue sky of the cloth.

In my hands the bottle sweats.
My thirst emptied it;
for now it is brimming with sun.
I could catch ladybugs inside it,
stuff it with grass.
But I am waiting.
The horse is approaching;
the wagon's approaching.
I will trade this
emptiness with the man
for milk my mother says
I need to fill up my bones.

Vocabulary

I

Whatever I bring into the house
rain or dry weather,
it is always mud.
Whether I wipe wet soles
of my tie-up black Oxfords
on the doormat after school
or track dust from the basement
down the front hall
I watch my footprints
sucked up into the vacuum,
nozzle nuzzling the floor
like a hungry puppy,
my mother dragged by it from one
room to the next,
restless, her hair coiled,
tight under a pink kerchief.

II

The vacuum is close by.
I hide in my room,
sprawl across polished hardwood
with the books I am
learning to read, the pages
anchored among the drafts
from under the door
by the steady
weight of my gaze.
I spy the dusty
path of a bookworm,
puzzle over the letters
that one after the other
slowly make names.

Some I already know the sound of,
my tongue sure of their shape
like the mudpies my hands
slap to the best
thickness in the back alley.

Already I use these names;
no one can make me
wash my hands of them.
I tuck them away
in my head like toys
to play with in bed.
After I am kissed goodnight
my light goes out and I am
telling myself stories
while no one is listening.
Sometimes I sing them
block letter by block.

III

Some words have meanings
no one explains.
Mud is a word my mother uses
for all things not clean.

IV

Tonight while washing
our dog's feet at the back door
I am telling him a story.
He's in from the rain.
I've knelt down beside him,
stroke his silky gold ears
dripping to the brim
of the beat-up yellow bowl
I plunge his paws into.

As I whisper,
mud loosens between the pads,
clots dissolving like magic
in the warm water,
the air through the screen door
muggy with earthworms.

I wipe the dog's feet
with a ravelling brown towel
that stiffens as it dries
in the hall cupboard.
No matter what stories I tell him,
he yawns, pulls away,
slides soggy-pawed down the linoleum.
I rinse the bowl;
mud settles
in the scratches his claws
cut into the plastic.

Setting

The knife goes here, the fork there,
the napkin a rigid triangle to its left.
The dessert spoon, the dessert fork
head to tail in a twinning
I have yet to figure out
above where a plate is about to appear,
above carrots in parsley, potatoes still boiling,
above sausages perfect with apple sauce.

Table edge cutting beneath the heart,
I place the gleaming
silver five times over
on starched yellow mats.
My mother straightens each setting.
From a cupboard above my head
she pulls out the wooden
salt and peppers that I forgot
because I couldn't see them,
because I should have asked.

Across the table they sit,
two sisters in ironed
blouses and pleated skirts.
One no longer lives here,
comes home from somewhere north.
The other once shared my bedroom.
We shared bunkbeds,
I slept beneath
among the shadows and dreamed of snakes,
my waking the venom
spreading up my legs.

Over dinner this sister laughs,
a wedge of light
fallen between Mum and Dad.
Through the window the sun
sinks, picking up

blood-red highlights in the mahogany
floating between the mats.

I start to laugh,
the joke aimed at my sister
dripping down my chin for all to see
in pulpy mouthfuls of carrot.
Fork over my head, hands blurring,
I clown in the faint
spotlight of the withdrawing sun.
This abandon knocks over
my glass of milk.

My mother turns her head;
her eyes narrow.

The silence of the house
darkens like a stain
in the tight
weave of the mat.
Silence darkens my family,
darkens the downcast of my sisters' eyes.
I am absent.

Mummy's little boy is locked
in his room.
He begins hurling books.
Laughter dies around the table,
the thin wedge of apple
pie worn down
on each half-eaten plate.

Book after book explodes
against the wall until the shelf
is empty, the boy drained,
knees folded up against his chest,
hands warmed by his aching
private parts, sobs
knotted against the hollow door.

Nails

A man is hammering his fingers
into the fence, nails red
and gleaming in the hot sun,
trigger-happy hammer-
head blurring, stuttering
loud bullets into the post.
I've opened the gate, knowing
only that I have been sent
into the alley to fetch him.

The hammer drives another
finger deeper into the fence,
the grain pocked with
bloody circles darker
than those under my eyes,
larger than the nickels
they give me on Sunday.

He smiles down at me.
I don't know his face
greasy with sweat,
don't know his arms
sticky with blood.
Whose arms lift me
in and out of the bath
and into my bed?
Whose fingers herd
animals across the wall
before the lamp at my bedside
snaps off?
I always forget what any
man's face looks like
disappearing into the dark.

The hammer shines in the sun.
I stand rigid,
ask him to stop, tell him
that Mother is calling.
The soup's getting cold.
Tears rip into my cheeks
like the raggy-toothed saw
hanging in the garage.
I have seen him use it,
squaring wood for my toybox,
plank after plank
astride the rickety horse
he never lets me ride.
As he works, the powdery
wood-flesh slowly rises
from the floor like an anthill.
I beat it down with a stick.

Why won't he stop fishing
into his pocket for spikes
pointed as nettles?
I am afraid they might bite.
I look down at my hands,
the nails tiny and clear
as the spread wings of bluebottles
I find hardening on sunny
window ledges all over the house,
six brittle legs always breaking
under the terrible
weight of my thumb.

He stands over me,
dark face haloed by sunlit cloud.
I look up to where his eyes
should be.
There is no place to run.

Who Is This

after a painting by Rachel Hesse

Mirrors hang against the tiled
alcove around the bath.
They cage the white triangle
of shirt buttoned
behind a cloud-grey suit,
triangle of white cotton
split by the abrupt line of a knotted tie.

The mirrors behead, sever legs,
a well-dressed torso that never leaves,
the face known only to the little boy
who sits round-shouldered
on the edge of the green bathtub,
the tiles reflected in the mirror behind him
feverish blue and purple,
his face upturned,
lips parted above a blunted jaw,
eyes knowing,
arms and legs goose-pimpled
climbing from the bath
that he was forced to run,
the bathroom window open,
penis shrunk into the folds
of his hairless scrotum.

Who is this man?
Why doesn't he wrap
the boy in the striped towel
hanging over the bath's edge
to dry him, to keep him warm?
Are these the sleeves
of a father's welcome arms?

Pre-Architecture

I

A country schoolhouse
on 21st Avenue N.W.
Two rooms in two storeys,
yellow paint flaking down from the eaves.
Decades of chalk shake
loose from the floorboards
as I step in, the door about me
a quadrangle of twilight
shadowed by the tall
buildings where my father
buses to and from work,
the net of streets paved,
spreading farther and farther
over the sold-off farms,
this old schoolhouse once
an oasis of honeysuckle and poplar
with two sets of swings.

II

I'm not the first to get here.
Shadows take the shape
of Akela stepping
from the teacher's office
in short pants like mine,
the hair on his thighs fuzzy
like tent caterpillars
under a magnifying glass,
their bodies squirmy with light.
Above the transom a dusty picture
where something like it
must have always been hung,
the smokey outline of one larger
frames this queen I have
promised to do my duty by

along with God who I am
sure always wears khaki
like Lord Baden-Powell;
he fought bores,
is wise in the lore of the jungle.
Akela smiles down at me
and straightens my cap,
stands framed by the door
like teachers before him,
feet firmly planted,
picking his teeth
with a blade of sweet grass.

III

Baloo saunters in, then Mang the bat.
The bandar logs in my six
tumble in, disturb the quiet
with scuffed shoes and unscrubbed paws,
claws torn and crusty with snot,
fangs and manes dirty,
fresh from soccer practice
but never ready for inspection.
I fall in with them,
tuck in my uniform.
Across the room, the flag
my *Cub Book* calls the Red Ensign
slumps, drags in the soiled
light like a coattail
on the floor.

IV

For my Modeller's badge
I have built a show home
out of styrofoam that my father
threw out, the blueprint

unfurling in my head as I cut
windows with a nail file,
pieced together doors
with toothpick hinges
from balsawood for a biplane,
filled each room with empty
spools for chairs,
matchbox beds and bits
of old fabric.
I boast that it is part
of a neighbourhood I want
to build up in the hills
beyond the city
with a view of the mountains.
The House of Raymour
I call it, ranch-style
with tumbleweed chandeliers
and a three car garage.

Upstairs the others are busy
at murder ball, the smack
of rubber against red
faces stinging my ears.

Bagheera stubs out his cigarette
as we sit in this damp basement
in two forgotten school desks.

He rubs the stubble
on his chin, sucks
at the motor oil the day
has worked into his palms.

He asks no questions.

V

I'm waiting on the porch,
the windows rattling behind me,
a lung collapsing in the night breezes;
my father is late.

Akela waits with me,
my hand warming in his,
the door to the school open,
the whole evening behind us,
the dust inside stirred up
like swallows wheeling
in the mouth of a barn.

Who knows who I will haunt,
my own yelling absorbed
by loose plaster when I try
to join games I am not sure of,

my voice years later still
half-heard among all the others
that struggle, slide from a crack,
whisper caution into the unprotected
ear of a boy like me stopped
like a heart, the ball
hurled out of nowhere.

Indian Graveyard, Gulf of Georgia, 1968

above in the cedars the bodies lie wrapped
in bark   beetles and rain
I cannot see them

other boys who risked the tricky
climb to each platform
flush with rumours of rags and grinning skulls
after supper   dusk and bones
of wood disappear into the smoke of the camp fire

we lie in a circle around the few embers

the sleeping boys I can see
are smiling   cold lips hardened
about ghost stories whispered moments ago
I did not hear them

wind like laughter climbs down through the trees

wave after wave repeats how we came
from one island over
stopping one night unlike those who stay
damp creeps into my toes and fingers

in the distance the glow of Vancouver
falters under the night sky as it swells
with constellations wheeling like goshawks

Physical

This hand —
what it uncovers, your breathing
as I examine you
downstairs in the airless basement, shirts pulled up
for the plastic stethoscope we should have
long ago outgrown, underwear and shorts
about our ankles, as we take turns
lying with knees
apart on my father's camp cot.

Already we seem older.
Hair wispy as your grandfather's
has begun to shiver where you want me
to probe you between the legs.
I run the cold
face of the stethoscope
below your bellybutton and listen —
your eyes follow my hand,
my lips tremble.

This is how we have come
to acknowledge the body, not through
words, which are dangerous,
but through touch and gesture, hours of playing
out the story of the patient
who does not get well,
a game we never tire of
as we search, play
with other boys, looking for cures.

It has begun to scare us how
the penis wakes
at random, freed from pants by zippers,
side by side, you and I
leaving in the snow one cold winter night
such signatures twined and steaming.

This hand —
it embraces mystery, the hungry
language of involuntary

nerve endings as I lie back on the cot,
not for the first
or last time, while above me
a yellow stethoscope that tells us
nothing
shimmers against your naked chest.

Stickmen

In retrospect, we can take comfort.
Something drew us together
that later could have torn us apart,
not just from each other, but from ourselves.
Who could have guessed back then,
two small boys caught in the rear
view mirror while your mother
drove, her eyes glancing toward and away
to the climbing road, my mother
in midsentence beside her, on the way
somewhere of their choosing
in the country, talking up a storm
past mountains, lakes, glaciers —
it seldom mattered.
Bulrushes blurred past us in ditches
overrun by spring thaw
and we were over our heads
in the weather of our own stories.

Sometimes they gave us crayons,
hoping we were bored.
What they would give now to open
a drawer crammed full
of our scrawled, unfettered longings,
have one still taped to the fridge.
How reassuring a drawing can be
of a stickman and stickwoman parked
in a red four door with stickchildren
in the back seat outside a house
with two windows and a door, smoke coiled
above a chimney slanted toward mountains
sharp and regular as cat's teeth.

If only they had recognized
early on a preference
for the colours that fill our closets.
Our punishment is to leave them
alone in our apartments
when they visit at Christmas.
They walk into our bedrooms
looking for shirts that need to be ironed.
The walls roil with unsettling
pictures, the night tables
cluttered with strong smelling
ointments and colognes,
issues of *10 Per Cent* and *Out/Look*
strangely open on the floor.
It takes them a long time
to notice that, fresh from work,
their red-cheeked sticksons
bend down to kiss them
with snow in their hair,
are actually smiling.

In retrospect, they must have forgotten
how in the basement of your house
we played with dolls pulled
from your sister's trunk of miniature clothes?
How unhappy we grew with my GI-Joe's lack
of anatomic precision, his muscular coldness.
How much more macho and silly
he seemed in Barbie's hiphuggers and blouse.
We told no one;
our games were for ourselves only.
We did not know yet about Paris
or that it could burn.

At fifteen we were stickmen awake
in the same bed for hours,
the late movie a love story
greasy and cold as our popcorn.
Such a close night, we stripped off our pyjamas,
the house with windows and locked doors
that I grew up in
asleep all around us.
We were afraid.
We were stickmen with sticks
growing where they weren't supposed to
between our shy legs.
We touched each other once
quickly; that was enough,
our sticks not yet used
to another's rough fingers.
How I wish we had become real
to each other in that northern suburb
where wilderness was so within reach
and risk a part of the landscape,
the bottomless lakes we dove into
at Scout camp, rockfaces and avalanches, bursts
of hail and sudden
chinooks that tear open rivers in February
icefloe by icefloe —
as our arms might have
had we held and kissed each other
to sleep that night, melted
even briefly the fear
and self-hate in our hearts.

In retrospect we can take comfort
that wholeness was ahead of us,
that together we walked part way,
that something we are proud to give another man
at last hangs between our legs,
that our lives include having friends
in our homes for dinner,
include lovers and drives in the country
include memory, knowing the land
becomes so unfamiliar at night
we no longer see it until something
in us changes, a return
to an earlier time of being lost.
Stars that never fail us
appear between the many branches
and suddenly we know our way.

Notation

I

A walnut RCA Victor
my parents bought second hand
long before I was born
sat out my childhood
on top of the basement wardrobe.
With string my father hooked it up
to the socket over his workbench.
One pull, then
music, *light*, the dial glinting
like yellowed walrus tusk
or the teeth of the old.

Now it attracts dust,
supports the indiscriminate
arms of an ivy reaching
for light in my study.

There is no point switching it on.
Some tubes, if unscrewed,
tinkle with spent filaments of metal,
their insides black and filmy like oil lamp chimneys.
Shadowing my progress about the room,
the silence is comfortable,
the conscience of a dead
relative at peace,
wandering, picking up static
objects that vibrate with use,
brass candlesticks shining through
a thousand past and future meals.

II

Notes to a song on the hit parade
that my father turned on,
a voice without a face giving
shape to words I couldn't yet know,
the diaphragm filling out each syllable
wistfully, desperately like pretend
maps of the unknown.

I would run over to the radio
in the kitchen, glass
of grape Kool-Aid clenched in both hands,
my heart suddenly too large,
rattling against my ribs
like a swallow tangled in a wind chime,
my tuneless voice caught up in the vortex
of someone else's emotion.

III

I listen to talk radio
Cross Country Check-Up taking up space
while I dice vegetables for curry,
my attention split by the knife.
The words I hear are shapes only.
Arranged logically,
like cans of tomato paste
and boxes of crackers growing
stale in the cupboard,
they exist to displace air,
air my lungs suck in, circulate
through my blood, then expel.
I listen to the radio;
words permeate
like molecules as I blend
cumin, mustard, turmeric, cayenne —
four words ground down
with mortar and pestle,
teasing my nostrils
while the radio flares.

IV

Past midnight,
safe under the covers
I would play my transistor,
tiny ventricle of darkness
pressed close to my heart,
flesh-toned headphone snug,
tapping my left ear.
The warmth of the blankets
drew everything much closer,
the voice of the DJ
deep and tender
yet remote like my father
down in the basement
silently reading through
a week's worth of the *Herald*,
the large pages unfolded
across the freezer lid or spreading
aside brushes soaking in varsol,
nails unsorted in cigar boxes,
scissors hovering, the blades parted
ready to snip out tidbits
on house repair or gardening,
perhaps an obituary,
glasses caught at the end of his nose.
Opera from New York
tinny in the distance,
always set the radio glowing.

V

Tonight I catch myself humming
with the refrigerator.
Its haphazard monotones give
shape to these atonal hours,
draw me away from my book
into the particular
cadence that is mine only,
notation I have yet to write down,
the arm of my turntable suspended
for a month in midsweep
above a record gritty, glittering with dust.
Whatever music I was born with
is quiet, difficult, and unnamed.

This Side of the Border

Alberta lies mostly on the interior plain,
its southern reaches dry
and treeless, flat to the untrained eye.
Outsiders drive quickly west,
seldom notice sloughs far
beneath skies of geese.
They pull off the Trans-Canada
at Brooks, picnic in the irrigated gardens
of the Experimental Farm.
A boy tips up a newly
opened rose.
              He breathes it in,
the scent vivid as the prairie wind.
He returns to the car, the rose
unlike him bred to withstand
the embrace of winter.

At the edge of each city, before
the poplar groves are ploughed under,
these green oases are rank with children.
Only these trees are old enough
to hold a child, shoulder
forts dreamt about in the school library,
the boards lifted from a half-finished house.
Unwanted jackets hung on lower
branches are thick with dust,
sunset sweating in the wind,
the call home for dinner
virulent as pollen.

Long ago surveyors walked the 49th parallel
past the Cypress Hills until they reached
the Rockies and struck northwest,
balanced along alpine ridges to an outlook
where, at the 55th parallel,
they grew tired of a view blocked
by misted peaks.
                    They descended,
cut north through
a parkland of scrub forest.
From Saskatchewan, the plains rose
to meet them,
                    foothills that chose
to kneel before them like
stepping stones.
                    They crossed the Peace and Spirit Rivers,
the day bitten with mosquitoes,
the rivers called to an ice-clogged ocean
beyond a border drafted one night
when, faint with cold,
                    they could push no farther.

Alberta lies mostly on the interior plain,
quarter sections paved for shopping malls
and highways.
                    In winter what is left
is open to masses
of continental polar air held at a distance
by block heaters and the Calgary Philharmonic.
Outsider beware.
                  What is brought from elsewhere
metamorphoses like pupae
caught among the weeds of Lac-des-Arcs.
The dragonfly that emerges has no name.
A child catches one downstream
in a mayonnaise jar.
It spreads damp wings.
The downdraft from holes driven
into the lid with hammer and nails
teases, barely keeps alive
all instinct of what these walls
of glass confine;
and of the river —
                  the current stirs up urges,
                  carries them along
                  to settle unnoticed in the shallows
                  of the river's more eastern dips and turns —

II   The City: Patriarchy

You can break your heart on all that you can
imagine, all that you can put out of your mind,
all that you can know.

Alan Barnett

In this club, some men cross over
the threshold by accident, out
for a good time with the boys.
With one or two beers in them,
they stand near the back.
As they get used to the glare
off the dance floor
out of the shadows the players
appear, bent over
cues in tight-ass jeans, the tips slippery
with chalk, brown eyes trained down a gleaming
mahogany shaft.
One provocative thrust
and the last balls sink into the welcome
grasp of a side pocket.
The winner is circled
by a lover's thick arms,
lips against lips, groin
grounded in groin.

How long have we waited for these
family men to stumble in here?
It has taken years to forget
the lines we practised so they would
never suspect us sitting among
the chosen at church, on the squash court,
in hospital, our bodies like theirs
in the efficient hands of a nurse.
Not long ago they began to ask
after our lives over a fast
cup of coffee between assignments at work,
between sets at the bench press
in the Body Works Studio.
These days we can talk with them less
discreetly about "friends," but why
should we trust them?

They envy our freedom,
our prospects, the money we spend.
We know they lift weights
with us for one purpose only,
to perpetuate the species,
their arms not yet strong
and steady enough to cradle
a baby so he won't wake.

They have forgotten that we are their brothers.
Like them, we are of man and woman born.
We repeat the same memories of Dad,
home late after work, lounging in a loosely-tied
robe, our feet dangling between
his furred legs while he asked
about homework, the games of chicken at recess.
He smiled down at us,
only the slant of his face altering
as we grew up toward him,
our chests filling out, our confidences
changing, our beards at last
rivalling his 5 o'clock shadow.

For him we learned to play hockey,
promised to become lawyers, looked
forward to a life with a mortgage.
But some of us grew afraid of his
raised hand, his disappointment.
Even then we were the ones who did
not want to fight any of his wars.
Instead we left home early, moved to Toronto.
Except for a few anxieties expressed long distance
and visits home alone during Christmas,
we have kept to ourselves.
But we can never forget him,
this straight man, the first man we loved.

Interior Design

> *And now our fairy*
> *decorator brightens his shop for fall;*
> *his fishnets filled with orange cork,*
> *orange, his cobbler's bench and awl;*
> *there is no money in his work*
> *he'd rather marry.*

> "Skunk Hour," Robert Lowell

The widows who want my help
are always melancholic,
mistake advice for interest.
It accrues daily, they think,
while for weeks we pore over wallpaper
samples and paint, endlessly unroll
blueprints for their empty ensuite bedrooms
or a deceased husband's den.
It is only work to me, inadvertent
flattery that dispels rumours scavenging
around me like gulls.
Otherwise I am seldom frank, chatter
away with them about far-off
children who are lured
home in a Chrysler full of kids
too soon after the fourth of July.

It is the young sons-in-law I like best,
the ones who are only a few years married.
They've left their baggy grey suits
with wide lapels in the closets of a Boston suburb,
the neatly hung trousers still damp with sweat.
On the dishevelled wake of their mothers-in-law
they ride into my shop in Bermuda shorts
and nylon shirts unbuttoned at the neck;
even the strayest of chest hairs
enticing against a light sunburn.

They are always full of smiles.
We nudge a few jokes past the old dears
and at what cost —
such exuberance buoyed by two weeks
away from the city and the boss.
I quiz them about the golf game.
Chests swell
and for a moment they forget
about wives building sandcastles
with sons at the ocean's edge.
For me this is enough,
though sometimes I chance upon them
among the dunes at midnight.

Local wisdom demurs that mine is not much
of a life, here in a seaside town,
especially off-season and so close to Maine.
A Korean War vet like me should have a woman
six months pregnant to redress my wounds.
Let them think what they like.

As usual the widows are making breakfast
for their children's children
in kitchens I have built,
their backs to views I argued them into,
cutting windows into their hearts
so they can watch the surf.
At sunrise I walk past them
and have the beach to myself
except for one or two lone swimmers
goose-fleshed in clinging bathing trunks.
I gather driftwood for the shop,
never cease to wonder why salt-smoothed
limbs of broken trees prove
tempting to the dowagers of Blue Hill;
flotsam is so easy to collect.

By noon the daughters have come
downstairs, calf-heavy with sleep,
spill coffee onto kidney-shaped tables
in an excess of bedroom laughter
I am sure is often at my expense.

Sometimes when the bay is calm,
I skip stones across the deep,
each stone skipping through names
of men I love until it sinks,
a chain of names that lengthens
each time I visit New York.
These names will never be wed
before the altar of the Covenanter Church
on Emerson Street.
A few join instead in our hearts,
Everett and Paul, Ben and Joseph,
names that last through time
and all the gossip.

After the Movies with O.

You emerged from the dark
of the cinema, trenchcoat
creased, face askew
under a beret that shadowed
eyes perpetually moving,
the crowd about you listless
under the lobby's thin light.

Someone introduced us and we began
talking, or you did,
fatherly hands blocking out
shot after shot in the movie.
You must have been past seventy.
Your rings hypnotized —
the marquee a haphazard
pulse of neon pulling
us into the night.

Sometimes we would have coffee.
Without asking questions
under the soft circle of light
lowered over our table
we spliced together
outtakes of our lives.

Mornings I would meet you
en route to the ocean
where you watched the Olympics
rise from the mist,
black aquiline peaks
breaching shyly as seals.
I never joined you,
though we often lingered
at May Street and Memorial,
the quiet path through the cemetery
down to Ross Bay an invitation
you walked out alone.

Where I went you would never know.
Yesterday I ran into a kid
who ripped tickets at the cinema.
Like me he knew you
only as O.
The last time he saw you
he couldn't recall, tagged you
as a wearer of loud ties —
livid slashes of colour.

Quel dommage, you'd say and laugh,
fading like a hologram into the darkness
that I move through,
in a different city
after the movies, on my way home.

Tonight Orion is out, his shoulders
perpetually squared.
Through the years he is
one companionable presence in the night
sky I recognize; I always map
the distant stars in his belt.

Who cared for you those last years
I will never know,
a prodigal afraid to return to an empty house,
your seat in the theatre filled
by someone else.
Who ripped your last ticket,
had coffee with you one more time?
Vaguely I remember you told me
that you once searched
through the telephone book,
never found my listing.

Parallel Lanes

We meet underwater, swimming in parallel lanes.
Both of us rising out of the breaststroke,
hands forcing the water apart.
We meet like this, length after length,
our trained bodies dreaming
a way to each end of the pool and turning,
coming up for air to breathe only,
the black hair matted across your chest
a flag that rises, that falls.

Later in the shower room,
after all the other swimmers have left,
we exchange something more furtive than glances,
something more gentle than words
as we talk, soap lathered onto our skins
and into our hair, washed
off with such pleasure, a common
language of bodies released from their stories
which we will tell each other over coffee
after we dress, underwear that is the beginning
and end of seduction, the well-worn jeans,
the red shirt that a sister made you
tucked in half-unbuttoned while drying your hair,
the dark flag of your chest unsettling
as you bend to lace up your runners.

On the steps of the Champagne Bath, we are suddenly ourselves.
Brightly coloured jackets resist the cold
air come between us as March blows off the river.
Walking into the Market, snow catches
in our hair like sparks, sparks that melt and go out.
Already you are telling me about some man
I will later watch you talk to,
leaning into the phone booth, laughing,
mouthing into the receiver: *I will be home soon*,
as you have been for eleven years.
Crossing a restaurant crowded
with empty tables and chairs with bashed-up legs,
you smile inwardly, navigate
among all the abandoned coffee cups
and the slow-burning candles between us.

Stripped of the heavy clothing of this snowy night,
I want to be held as the water holds you,
swimming in another lane towards and away.
I want to hold this man of yours as you do,
want to know, in one lasting embrace, how to hold a man
forever in the sure arms of this, my only life.

Lives of the Saints

I

The river tonight
runs cobalt, swans caught in the veins

of undercurrent, a surfeit
of calm as we meet

on a far bank
and talk, walking between

shafts of darkness and moonlight.
In a city park, night

is a maze of trees and men
pausing by the river, a trail of glinting

cigarettes followed
from one cavity of shadow

to the next,
privacy hollowed out, flamed

and fringed with leaves
by matches quickly

struck before eyes in recesses,
men remote and virile as saints.

II

Who am I to talk
of sainthood? A lamentation

of swans is caught up in the metaphor
of our lust, our hands

join in the unobserved
darkness, question

why we are here.
Will you ever see me, I say

with my eyes, what I look
like, my intent, here

in the sacred grove,
among the ghostly maples,

your body heavy against mine
though we may never know

much else of each other
beyond this park and the cold

ecstatic blue
potential of this citified river.

III

Hope is what we drown in
as you baptize

me in the sheets of your bed,
belief that the body

transforms into something
we can live with,

a prayer, a memory, a continuing
presence we might wake

beside, serve breakfast.
Someone who likes to exchange

words for no reason,
who can tolerate

poetry and assumes the same patterns
of the body, how

a mug is held, an eyebrow
twisted, cock curving

into a lover's palm like the long
subtle neck of a cob, a man

who shaves and has a life of his own,
who accepts gains and loss

shared by two men in a bed neither
claims as purely his own,

two men who run
with the dog through the park

at twilight, the fathomless
blue river flowing past

toward darkness, two men
feeding the swans.

IV

The breadcrumbs offered
go stale too quickly,

we lose our way in the forest
other men tried raising

a fence around with curfews
and streetlights,

prophecy to keep us out or in.
Even still night never comes

to an end early enough
for us to find our way home,

boredom sets in while we wait,
smoking cigarettes,

unable to stay warm.
Desire can be boring.

Take you, for instance,
you're all for wine

at dinner, but nothing domestic.
So here we are again,

by the river, tracing movements
intricate as fireflies,

profane stratagems.
And though our names

keep changing,
our bodies do not.

At least not yet.
Old stories run fast,

swans strangely calm,
afloat on the aftermath.

Ripper

When they found chocolate dripping
from your fingers, the factory
let you go; the city health code
could not allow for dead skin
caught under ragged nails
to loosen into the fragrant vats.
The foreman had to warn you
once too often, shake you
from a dream where we swam
across endless baths of milky darkness,
our limbs bits of coated nougat
that melt to nothing on your tongue.
In the factory heat your work clothes
stank of piss and chocolate.

The foreman let you go;
now you wander the lakeshore,
stop in clubs where men meet men,
men who want to be held, to be something
sweet and lasting in another's arms.
You dance with us, buy us drinks,
sometimes offer rides home.
Our way is the direction
you are always going.

Your cupboards are full of spilled
Frye's Cocoa and Nestle's Quik,
are full of bones sucked clean.
In the utensil drawer, ribs
are kept separate from the metatarsals.
Under the sink stand mason jars
of testes dated in grease pencil
like your mother's preserves.

Shoe boxes in the bedroom
bulge with pictures of the still
living and the newly dead,
mementos that record the evolution
of each disembowelment;
you want to know
us repeatedly from the outside in.

The authorities will blame us
when they find our heads softening
like lettuce in the crisper,
our enucleated eyes staring
in surprise at them from a freezer
tacky with chocolate ice cream;
you never took time to defrost.
Some handsome young officer
who works up a sweat nightly
at the gym, will scald his right
hand reaching through the steam,
turning off the heat beneath
a pot of swelling biceps
pumped up larger than life.

For days, callers to on-air
call-in shows will claim such passion
is a sickness, that the cold
blood burning through your veins
is tainted like ours
and those like us
still haunting the streets,
that Milwaukee must not ignore us
any longer, though the police
ignored how you dragged
one of us escaped and bleeding
back to your tenement on State Street.
Your arm resting on his shoulders
reassured them.
The case was closed.

How that boy first came to be
in your apartment only
we who came before him will ever know.
Others will insist on asking
if it was the force of your desire
or merely force.
For them like you he is one
among many, a life
you deconstructed like a sociologist
or a mechanic salvaging parts,
our deaths a preparation,
like a recipe for éclairs,
for the perfect man or the perfect victim,
our black against your white skin
such bitter chocolate.
We are men you never loved,
whose families, until they read
the paper, never knew why
we did not come home.
Until this morning, over coffee,
they seldom talked
about us, never said our names.

For the Boy with the Eyes of the Virgin

Let me be your ice,

the boy says in the Texas heat,
black mestizo eyes,
broad face, bare-chested, barely sixteen,

says this to me
near Losoya and Commerce,
where I have been approached before

by a black mother for bus fare, an exhausted
daughter cranky in her arms,

in the hotel district, overlooking the Riverwalk,
its paved water-level
pathways flooding with tourists, flowers, and noise,

an attempt at urban renewal
where lovers meet
beneath the pecan trees after store owners
roll down the protective metal grills.

This boy offers to cool me down,
on a day hotter than blood,

when, dehydrated and sunstroked,
all I want after hours

of pilgrimage to the four
tumbledown stone missions which give this
lonely city some kind of heart

is something cold —

I will take almost anything,
having stopped at this
snow cone stand where he seems to have
waited all afternoon for someone
dazed and weary, ribbing

the girl who works it, who tries
to block him from me;
the scooped-out globes of crushed ice
she gives me for so little
staining my tongue cherry-red.

This cone of mired arctic
purity smoking
in my hand barely slakes
my thirst and the boy follows

as I move on, wants to
guide me wherever it is I want to go,
back to my hotel if need be.
Let me be your ice,
mister, you're so hot, you better lie down.

The scored veins of his arms
are clotted with stigmata,
this smooth-chested
boy with the eyes of the Virgin
of Guadeloupe whose gaze,
sun-crazed, I felt
follow me from nave to nave down the poorly
marked Mission Trail and last night

in the bars along San Pedro.

Dark-eyed men who flew with the USAF
the only time they left Texas.
Their looks make my blood
tingle with cayenne, these grounded
flyboys who like to two-step at the Silver Dollar,
who joyride in pickups after hours
all the way down to the Alamo.

And this is where I leave him,

at the monument to Col. Travis and Davy Crockett
and the 189 white patriots
who were not the only ones to fall.

Something marketable in San Antonio's history
not lost on him
as he starts to explain,

this aggressively beautiful boy
who, as the twilight
breezes lift stray
newsprint from the gutter,

looks hungry as well as cold,

who I refuse with money, not knowing what
icy current of death
he might carry in his blood.

Impotence

When you threw me from the cliffs
at Majors' Hill Park,
did you watch me fall?
Or was the power in your hands
enough, grabbing me about the waist,
the relaxed twist of my spine
under thin t-shirt cotton
tensing, trapezium alive
to the sudden hardness of your chest,
my body already falling
back into your arms.
You spent me like the change
in your pocket, spilled
me through the dark
closing about me as I arched
downward, breath torn
and fading from my lungs, emptied
like the wallet you stole,
my name enduring
on worn-down plastic cards
which you used
once, then threw away.

All summer the papers said the fallen
men found at dawn near the canal
below Parliament Hill were drunk,
fell to wish-fulfilment deaths.
The same August night you
and your buddies chased
another man whom you found
too good-looking
across the Alexandra Bridge,

stripped him
of his money and his rings,
beat him over the head with a stick,
kicked and fought over him
until at last one among you
took his life in hand;
"nice shoes," someone said,
and over he went.
The police took photos
of frogmen freeing
his body from among the pilings.

Still later that night
your gang forced in
the door of a suburban home,
two men woken and disentwined
from sleep by screwdrivers
and knives tearing more
deeply into them than any
eyes they would meet on the cul-de-sac
hauling in groceries each Saturday
or arriving home like newlyweds
in the same car from work,
more than bachelors, not quite single
fathers with weekend kids.
One escaped and bled across the lawn,
lost consciousness
in a neighbour's uncomprehending arms.

A young offender in adult court,
you stand before the jury
with evidence you are afraid to give.
You fear how some men love
each other through the body.
You are powerless: our bodies
are too like your own.

You fear your every gesture,
and the face in the mirror,
its delicate lines you tried
to shave away by dropping
out of high school and living on the streets.
We'd see you with your friends
in the shopping malls, lean young men
in leather, with erratic hair
and narrowed faces.
You'd watch us pass by
on our way to the movies.
Even with your back turned on us,
you hated how your jeans
tightened across the ass.
You always thought that you
caught us looking,
swore that the muscles
you charged up with push-ups
were never meant for us.

Physical Education

The body I wear now
you refused when we were in school,
you with your leather glove, out in left field.

Standing over the plate, the bat
heavy on my shoulder, anxious
to be struck out, I swung,
aiming for a home run to make you
stumble as you leapt for the catch.

But my arms were matchsticks.
You liked to snap them behind my back
to make our friends laugh.

Squeezing the bat, I prayed
my body would transform
on impact with the ball
so I could speed to first
base as DiMaggio
or walk there as a girl
whose poise seemed natural.

But the ball always whizzed
past or winded me.
You stood above me as I lay
in the mud, catching my breath.

Through bruised eyes I'd watch you,
my fear blinding as hardball.

❖

Yours is a body I have come
to love with the love
and fear of a man who has
come to love and fear men.

I did not know this in the locker room
as you peeled off a towel
and stepped under the shower,

all of us soaping down and trying
not to see how water steamed
about your shoulders,
pooled along the collarbone,
and flowed down your chest,

water corkscrewing off the tip
of your penis luxuriantly as piss.

I was envious, but did not know this,
knew only that to meet your eyes,
or the eyes of others, always brought
laughter, comparisons, and jokes

about the smallness of my balls,
the thinness of my legs.

Once, after we had left school,
I held you in my arms
and you did not push me away.
We had been drinking,
having met in a hotel lounge by chance.

How I managed to undress you,
how you managed to take
my cock in your mouth with such care

I will never guess, know
only how you sucked
at my nipples like a newborn,
then, still hungry,
how you drew me inside you,
my stomach sliding
against your lower back,

how I came too quickly,
having wanted you for years,

how this anomalous knowledge
of our bodies
for one night put aside anger,
how for one night we fell asleep
in a tangle of white sheets and semen

to wake disentangled and apart,
two men who would never
hold each other the same way,
and at last knew themselves
as equals, unencumbered by guilt.

❖

Tonight you are standing outside the diamond,
legs and arms primed for the next play,
while the lilacs in the park around you
echo with the calls of blackbirds
settling down for the night, the flames
of their wings folded close to their bodies
as the sky deepens beyond twilight.

In the stands beside me your girlfriend
leans forward to catch the last
flicker of birdsong on the wind while we chat.
Suddenly the man up to bat hits one
into left field and the two of us
are entranced and obliterated
by the smash of wood against leather,
with the pitch of your body atwist
under your sweaty t-shirt as you
catch, drive the ball into home plate.

The play is over; your girlfriend
talks about how the red blur
of blackbirds between day and night
is sexual, how the sky blooms
with dusk, how it makes her
flush to think of your hand
reaching up inside your glove.
I lose track of what she is saying
as you begin taunting the next batter
with insults I remember from high school.

Even back then they were bluff,
though often I forget, still afraid
your eyes will harden as they used to,
afraid you will force me to my knees
behind the backstop, your girlfriend
laughing at me, her arm about your waist
as you walk away in the bloody evening light.

Suddenly you wave up at us,
your hand ungloved in the dusk,
the palm so open with love
it still makes me nervous
as the wind picks up, easing
the blackbirds from the lilacs —
they wheel calmly, red wings
charting the interstices
that grow between men at night.

Best Man

You ask me to stand
for you while you go down
on one
      knee, the woman
you love beside you, your life
together open

like a Bible before the Justice
of the Peace and invited
guests in the Jasper Room of this refurbished
railway hotel, its richly
appointed suites overlooking the crooked,
custodial arm of the North Saskatchewan
whose current once bore the girth
of York boats provisioning the fort,
bearing whiskey, beads, and the future
city no one could have guessed at.

Someone named this four-star
baronial monstrosity after an alcoholic

prime minister from the east
of this country where we live almost
100 years after his death, the father
of a confederation whose laws
relish joining
you as one body with this woman

while I stand to one side, watching, vicarious

celebrant, best man who loves
men no better than myself

and no worse off, our commitment to each
other sanctified only by our own
kisses and obsessions with flowers,

by our privately observed
pledges that often bind us blindly;
no laws extant
that protect us from the lawless
passions of a passion gone wrong.

Though we live next door in the highrises staggered
above Victoria Park Road, share the same views

of the High Level Bridge at sunrise,
first light clarified by the gliding
panes of our unlocked patio doors.

Though we loiter with the rednecks
at Commonwealth Stadium, cheer for the running
backs or any other backs turned
cheekily toward us by the Edmonton Eskimos.

Though we pay taxes.

I stand with you, your best
man for the evening,
drinking your new wife's champagne,
remembering not to catch her
bouquet as I improvise

on the toast to the groom,
choosing words from among many,

inspiration spooled up for the record
by a camcorder hand-held by some
in-law whose name I forget,

ad-lib that for a split second
places me at the centre

of your life as you both spin
between old and new,
my words not to be forgotten by mothers and fathers,
by sisters, brothers and friends
who all day have asked
after the girls in my life,
their eyes wondering
about me as I stand
and for the first time know

friendship, its power

to curse and to bless.
My words fill this
room just as someday, in my name,
I hope you will stand
in the nervy limelight, wishing me the same
chance at love, in a ceremony
and a city of my choosing, its charter

rewritten in the purest syllables
of the language,
no longer a hinterland civics of difference and fear.

For Magie at the Bedside of Her Dying Friend

Magie at the bedside of her dying friend,
a man she dressed one night
for a part in *Cats*.
She fit him into his cat-skin;
he told her about the new man he'd met.

Magie sits close, waiting,
in surgical gloves and mask.
He lies strapped to his bed,
body thinned beyond frailty
skin loose as any costume
she would alter
to make him look his best,
fingers too weak to turn
the pages of death's well-worn script,
sedated beyond dementia's prompting,
the agony of forgotten lines.
She remembers other men she's lost:
dressers at the Met, actors,
waiters, set designers,
best boys she'd meet
for lunch near Sheridan Square.
The cold wind blowing down
the Avenue of the Americas
each winter never worried her.
New York was a great city
and she had a part in its theatre.

Twenty-six men she has watched die
and now the script is out-of-date.
She writes pamphlets, joins marches
while other men work on Wall Street,
make decisions in City Hall,
catch trains in the evening
at Grand Central, indifferent,
bored, not looking out the window
at the drama of falling
leaves, the burnt
golds flooding backyards,
passing through Westchester,
the comics and the Business Section,
picking up the car, home
for a late supper, then to bed,
unafraid of what they might pass on
to their wives whose legs wrap
around them, holding them inside
as they come; that split second
of ecstasy makes them feel safe

while Magie sits in darkness
beside another man who loved
with equal ardour, counting his last breaths.

The Aqua-Nuns

Not yet out of view as we clear
the pool, nuns with downcast eyes
wait by the shallow end,
shy giggles held back by hands
skilled at devotion.
Hands which care for the ill
stretched these swimsuits over bodies
that years ago were married to Christ.
Here, in tangerine and chartreuse,
no one could mistake them for brides.
Bathing caps pulled on like haloes
shine under the skylight.

Glancing back discreetly at these ladies,
we climb out of the pool, spirited
away by lifeguards who, like young gods
in flesh-toned shorts and open-necked shirts,
cloister us by sex into the heat of the showers.
We soap ourselves down and laugh,
the chlorine we worked our way
through, swimming lap after lap,
pours off our bodies like sweat.

The second the locker room doors close,
this is the ritual:
the pool's music changes —
The Dance of the Sugar Plum Fairy
perhaps or *L'Après-midi d'une Faune.*
Buoyed by blue lifebelts, the nuns
one by one take to the water.
They wheel about like ducks, at bliss
in circles that expand and contract,
upending like synchronized swimmers,
unselfconscious ankles out of their element,
unpainted toenails aglitter in fluorescent light.

We can't help envying their freedom
of movement; they have been released
from lanes that during the Adult Swim
divide us, swimmer from swimmer,
slow from fast, awkward from svelte.
The barriers like snakes laze
coiled and tempting on the deck
which, as children, we were told
never to run across, snakes chasing us
with longings we have never escaped.
Vainly we stretch our bodies
before swimming, stretch
muscles that we work hard for,
wearing swimsuits that fit some of us
snugly, barely covering crotches.
For these women, their escapes
are made already.
For them, this oblong of water is holy.
They don't need an imposed structure
of desire to get them in shape.

Artificial Intelligence

This is the inheritance.
Coded in binary

and stored in far-off databanks,
all the mind evolved toward

lives at last free of the body,
the skin a loose-fitting

envelope that time has discarded.
Yet unsure of its origins

the brain, in this post-human age,
notes a strange absence.

Reading files called up
from memory, it registers

an emptiness
unfulfilled by any algorithm

of how pleasure once
emerged from the juncture

of soft and disparate flesh,
or how afterward, while one slept

his other settled in the kitchen,
hair-flecked fingers around a mug of coffee,

the direction of thought snagged
up in the plot of some mystery,

the novel by Ruth Rendell open on the table,
its pages turning red in the late evening light.

Desire
is now plotted only on graphs,

simply documentation
of what it is to be human —

in one file: walks that take a man away
along the banks of the Ottawa River after twilight,

autumn approaching the Gatineau Hills
in the purple mask of the first cold night;

in another: a memory, as he falls
asleep, of his boyhood

bedroom, the ceiling lamp clicked off,
his older sister disappearing into the glow

of a door left ajar,
the next morning sudden as his eyes, opening.

Such images are data only,
combinations of 0 and 1.

Where are the fathers,
the mothers (whoever you like) —

the lost programmers who failed to enter
enough in the help files

to interpret what needs to be
processed, the story

half-forgotten
as it was logged in.

Patriarchy

How long does it take to grow
into the bodies handed down to us
at birth, each an accident
of chromosomes, mysterious
to our mothers as they held us,
laughing, lifting us high in the air,
our feet kicking at their amazement
with us, little boys who forced
a way out between their legs
with bodies so unlike their own.

Even then, they saw us as alien,
like our fathers who lay
comfortably beside them in bed, wearing pyjamas.
Even your father, a pious man standing
in the pulpit of the Baptist Church,
had something to hide under his vestments
that made them feel restless.
At random it grew forbiddingly rigid,
Deuteronomy, The Ten Commandments,
babies, babies, babies,
and *The Epistles of Saint Paul*.
The boys in Sunday School watched
snow pile up outside a window
hot with our breathing, hankered
wistfully after a puck sliced across
Tri-Wood Rink by their sticks.
I wanted to cut mine off —

What a relief: in the middle
of soccer practice, someone
would yank off my gym shorts and I'd win
instant respect, discovered
at last for what I was or wanted to be,
someone special, regal as any
full-blooded queen.
After school, while our mothers
shuffled cards and drank
tea in the kitchen,
we played downstairs
under a bald light bulb swung
low over the washer and dryer.
Swathed in unwashed sheets,
we couldn't wait to grow
into my sister's unthreatening
bras and nylons, our boys' faces
masked under accretions of rouge.

Falling asleep, I'd imagine
the sleek, hairless bodies of men
without faces who formed a circle
around my bed and seduced me
for my subversive feminine charms.
Yet I never imagined exactly,
never felt breasts ache
with milk for an unwanted child
or a vagina torn and bleeding
from unasked for, repeated intrusions
by men whose faces, if I were
truly a woman, I could never forget.
Though I was only nine then,
this memory haunts me,
a dark form that shadows me home,
waits beneath my window in leather
and a brushcut as I move
without having the mail forwarded

from address to address.
Half willingly, half afraid
the last time I saw you,
I sought refuge in your arms.
But your passion overwhelmed me
with envy, you more able than I
to admit to the desires we shared.

Now I stand with a man you will
never meet, outside a circle
of women keeping vigil,
guilty tears in our eyes as we watch them
lay down flowers in the November rain,
roses, carnations, birds of paradise,
spring bulbs planted for a woman
hunted down as she was walking to work
by a man who once said
he loved her, who she once had believed,
who shot her yesterday morning near this downtown park,
not with Cupid's arrow,
but with a crossbow straight through the heart.

Standing behind these women,
I grasp the hand
of the man beside me with a hand
that has known violence,
has felt the heat-flash of leather
in a classroom, then closed
round it in a fist.
Years later I put this fist through
a window in anger, my thumb
partially numb ever since,
ready to fight off any masked
or unmasked man who might
surprise me, leaving a bar
one late and starless night.
I grieve how brutally I turned
against you, rose from your bed
the next morning and discarded you.

This is the patriarchy that I thought,
in loving men, I would escape —
my hand linking with another's
until now for all the wrong reasons.
Among these women, the body
of the man beside me is
ordinary and free for all he can hold,
not just in his arms,
but for the story inside
that no longer needs to be his alone.
Now that I am ready to listen, maybe he will
tell me everything
as it was from the beginning.

Touch

Pastry spreads from my fingers
like history, like braille.
The edges thin under the practised
weight of a marble rolling pin,
the dough opening from the centre.
With a knife I caress,
ease out the final circle,
pat it into a glass pie plate.

Shell after shell I make
while you watch.
The touch my mother gave me
is in my hands as they form
dough into a ball,
the secret society of pastry
passed down from parent to child.
Male or female, it doesn't matter,
though many times a boy
has watched his mother spin
globes of dough into sudden
reservoirs of pleasure
on her sun-warmed countertop.

My gift is this shaping,
this tactile instinct
for shortening and flour.
It moulds to whatever form
you give me, turns golden
around whatever we want it to hold.

Vernix

I

Two masks wrapped in the unreadable
crumple of a Chinese daily —
a gift sent by a friend in Jinan.
Ideograms rub off on my fingers
as I lift out these nested
papier-mâché ovals with elastic
head straps and cut-out eyes.

In a mirror I am the moon
with eyebrows plucked,
and lips rouged, skin serene
as egg white, forehead
in the last quarter shyly
throwing back light.

Monkey-king fits too snugly.
An ironic fellow, red-faced
behind a ruff of matted brown hair.
I can't take him too seriously.
My temples ache, jaundiced
by his unregal despair.

I prefer my own face,
how it changes
from one moment to the next, felt
in the expressions of those I greet
on the street or the men
beside me in bed.
How one might turn
toward me or another away.

Or how in the morning Eric
brews tea, halves grapefruit
but Mark sits in impatient
silence at the table
and wants to be fed.

Nothing is fixed, nothing endures

except these features, the bone
structure comfortable under
layers of skin ready to age,
the nose my mother lent me,
the motes left in both eyes
by my father's gaze.

II

I rearrange the masks
on my wall, rearrange
the thoughts I have collected
about them over the years.

The old year mask from the Andes . . .
The carver should have
made himself another, burned this
rough shell at the New Year.
His soul is unpurified,
for as long as this likeness
hangs in my living room,
the misshapen eyes, splayed
nose, and slow grin
that he carved as a charm
against bad omen
chiselled inside him till death.

The clay countenance of a woman
looking downward,
its Jamaican artist famous
living above Kingston
with his daughters in the Red Hills.
The woman's face is sullen,
her skin washed-out
terracotta, the patina
of her iconization: *Miss Jamaica* —
woman looking downward
in deference to a man,
eyes not quite closing.

The mask from the Great
Lakes of East Africa,
two ventricles of fresh water
draining a continent.
Here, in this place where I live
I know least about hunger,
about this ebony face hanging
disembodied near a window.
A knowing passionate light
wells up from the grain.
Skin like this should be oiled
with scent, hair pulled
back into intricate braids.
This woman should have
two healthy children
hanging from her arms,
her earlobes elongated
by their fingers yanking
at her earrings,
her valuables
this boy and girl, the life
she can give them.
I want to know this woman.

Among these masks I hang
the gifts from China.
They performed intrigues
in the Shandong Opera only
my friend knows something of,
illusions she sent me
to consider from halfway
round the world.
They lure me with their beauty.
Curiosity is never less,
never more than a second skin.

III

These are the masks of my country
dug up in the landfill,
mired under layers of second-hand time.

Ski masks and a welder's mask,
the mask of a goalie tangled
in the veil of a forgotten bride.

A surgeon might have worn this
while I was under, having counted
backward as far as possible,
on the way to my beginning.
He leaned over me, cut free
my appendix under the harsh lights,
this mask a moist membrane
of linen between us, between
his breaths, screening out chance.

And down farther: the black
mask of a sleeper who woke
refreshed in late afternoon
beside me and I ripped
it off, the elastic holding
back dreams I was thirsty
to share, which spilled
and evaporated, the sleep
I emptied him out of,
a bottle forced open.

The nightmare of the bal masqué,
the guises worn at school
dances from junior high onward,
that leered (or seemed to)
under the strobe lights
with the music from one hit
single to the next, the t-shirts
and ripped jeans, faces
anxious, across which played
the rise and fall of our make-up.

And deeper: the masks worn
at Halloween transforming
the neighbourhood
with other kids once a year
just before nightfall,
our mothers waiting at the end
of the sidewalk while we climbed
strange steps, half hoping
to be found out, to be recognized,
the risk worth the treat.

IV

At bottom, to live without masks
is to deny the unconscious,

to deny how it forms
in nanoseconds, sperm and ovum
bonding, nesting
each inside the other, making
one emptiness, an inland
sea of chromosomes that lifetimes
are spent catching
sight of, fish we want to give names.

The fetus wears the womb
bravely; the walls stretch, harbour
a world of growing particulars.
Layer upon layer of torn
newspaper, the mother
glues down tentative
strips of longing
about the baby, love
pasted over anxiety, over
fragments recalled browsing
the *Citizen* each morning —
recipes for winter baking,
Sputnik and Elvis,
the homeless weathering cold nights
in caves under the Houses
of Parliament —
her desire compulsive,
hardening, strip after
strip about this
life imploding inside her,
the womb a mask assumed
on the way toward
gender, fingers and toes,
laughter and eyes that see all.

The features of this mask
are moulded by the first
tentative kicks, the world felt
from the inside out, but
from the outside little is known
until this intense piñata
breaks open
in a torrent, the body
weighed and set going with a slap,
the placenta sloughed
like a deflated balloon.

A moon in white and waxy eclipse,
the vernix caseosa is sponged gently
away and the face wears
a new mask, wears the unfamiliar
light of first morning, wears the shine
of a mother's eyes as she shows him off,
as she croons and brags.

V

Thirty-four years later the body
gets up in the morning,
without thinking begins to pick up its clothes,

assembles the day ahead
before the mirror after showering.
No one else can wear it the way I do.
No one else has the flare
for these pants from Italy that crease
round my crotch, this lavender
shirt from Hong Kong,
its parachute loose about my ribs.

Caught in the mirror, I wear
the room behind me,
in my eyes its sunlight and disorder,
its African violets and family portraits
perpetually smiling, the cacophony
of half-read books open and face down
like masks on the night table,
the themes long ago worn
out and done with.

What story needs to get told
depends less on words than on signs,
depends on what is encrypted on my face

by the man who sat across from me
last night in a restaurant.
What is it that I am reading in my eyes
this morning as I rub,
consider this unshaven face, an unceasing
mask of maleness I did not ask for
and can never discard,
though I lift it off daily
in a blood ritual of water and soap?

Today I claim it as mine.
I read its potential
for rousing a new lover's thighs.

I assemble myself, knot a tie scavenged
from the depths of Filene's basement in Boston.
The Navajo ring my sister gave me,
I slip it on for luck.

The man across from me last night,
we tried on conversation.
The food we shared became more
than the flavours of lemon grass and Vietnam,
more than the ruined temples along the Mekong
described on the menu,
more than the masks stripped from them
by looters, the iridescent faces reproduced
and sold in the market to tourists.

Today I assemble the man and his stories.
I want him to lift off
the mask of desire I gave him,
if possible, and show his own face.
Though I collect and discard
the days of my life, I only let go
of what is not truly mine.
I try on each moment before the mirror;
each memory that is kept,
though it fits like a mask,
I put on and take off
with little hesitation, whatever spell
such brief wearing casts.

III THE HINTERLAND: ECOLOGY

the same boy sent to his room for punishment
leans from his window listening for animals
far away in the woods strains his ears to catch
even the slightest sound of rage but nothing howls
even the hoot of owls in the dusk is gentle

Anne Szumigalski

Mnemonics

Fir cones on wet pavement,
unopened, innocent as dung,

draw into themselves,
small creatures chastely cabined.

With scant malice
the wind felled them quickly

like a commuter train passing on.
Mulched leaves

disintegrate beneath them,
pooled bits of maple

and cotoneaster
flamed by last night's abrupt frost.

Nearby a neighbour's bonfire
stutters; it's no use,

nothing erases
evidence of our inward

turning, the passions slowed.
Rain

dripping from stripped branches
sows itself

conspicuously
into the brain's furrows.

Each time I pick up a fir cone
compulsively the mind

makes a fist around it,
thinks *fir cone*,

perhaps *ovoid*,
the life within such

afternoons leaving
teeth marks in my palm.

Noise

You try to block it out with music
with a fan treading stale air, blades snarled

in the currency of unrestful nights, windows
closed against buses endless

and grumbling across the Cummings Bridge.
Voices from below —

one punctuates the other's rise
to climax, she can't help it or his chest

tightening without your permission under white
t-shirt cotton as he soaps down

the car every weekend in shorts below
your window, you can't deny

it, can't deny his butt, how haired
and silky it must feel beneath her fingers.

Close your eyes,
but try as you might, you can't

wait for them to finish, can't wait for someone
to step in, take his place, fill the blank

space inside that you never admit
is there no matter what

word you choose to name it, to block it out.
Words change, no longer describe

taps running hot and cold, sex, the deluge
of spring birds and memory; but

they are indivisible, human noise and the roar of nature.
Love or lose them both, the river's thaw

here and another break-up over two thousand miles
and twenty-five years away, your sense

of family far and fragmentary as the ice floes
melting, floating down

stream below your window as you wait for
silence, silence and kites.

As a boy you blocked the gutters
of your street with dams

of snow, runoff boiling up behind.
You loved it, the sense of power

to hold back, to resist.
Now you feel powerless, everything gets in

no matter what, loneliness, love
weightless as a mouse squeezing through

a hole the width of its jaw,
dragging its elephantine appetite

upward through your walls, your veins.
Open the window, let it all in,

let it out, you can't help it, the stale air,
your human voice, the roar: of nature.

Together in the woods
for the first time in years,
we discover red trilliums
like helicopters
landed among the ferns,
beneath maples, the young leaves
like fists uncurling
sunward, porous as lace.
We talk as we once did,
mother and son,
ignore words that hurt us,
the shield that glaciers
broke down into slivers
of gravel slipping
into our shoes.

In wet ditches of this
Ontario highway I have driven
with pleasure all summer:

first milkweed insinuating
through bulrushes,
then late flowering ragweed,
then golden glow which grew
in Alberta untamable
near our garage door.
I used to watch you prune,
tie back its unruly stalks.

Tiny flies you could never
rid yourself of
nagged at the yellow blossoms,
a singing cloud of wings
condensing over the patio
while we itched through twilight
insistently reading,

this desire for words forever
identified with pain.

❖

Home for my holiday
you drive me west,
a book of Rocky Mountain flowers
colour-coded and open
in my lap.
The view from the car
leafs through it, through us.
What can we do with this
excess of poetry?
Greedily, we name
species at random.

Binoculars and a camera
in the back seat,
you want to catch each minute,
keep me here long after
I have left.
Years it has taken me to accept
that in this landscape I am still,
like the grasslands,
a windswept presence.

C-Level Cirque

I have finished your sentence,
skilled at interrupting your struggle
against silence with any word
that might coax what is inside
you into the open.
Words mark
territory in the wastes of conversation
I have learned to recognize
as ours.
      The reserve and flux
of temper shift like winds
off the eastern slopes of the Rockies,
each gust more violent as it drops
toward Calgary, boiling
up the snow whenever
we drive across Morley Flats
headlong into a blizzard.

Your face, your eyes relax,
lips letting go, smoothing over your teeth;
I have said the right thing.
My tongue rests more
certainly inside the saline
wash of my mouth as I breathe,
feel myself think: this silence
is different; it holds
us like a car with a destination,
a plateau we can reach.

Soon words whistle from us
as we hike above Lake Minnewanka
into a cirque some glacier emptied
itself out of.
      Words hang
in the currents like hawks,
defying absence until one of us
shouts.

Words scatter against ice-shorn granite.
Like squalls of bird cries,
each syllable returns to us shattered,
the cirque a weathered cranium,
an imperfect soundbox for the voice
filling with echoes that overlap.
The wind, not hearing the words it speaks,
interrupts itself, stutters.

Love hesitates between father and son,
knocks at the throat,
often seizes like an engine.
We idle in the parking lot at trail's end;
mugs of coffee sit on the dash,
steam rising, carrying away warmth.
Words lodge between our ribs
like fog in remote passes.

Sometimes we stay closer to home,
let the dog run free
in fields no longer browsed over by cattle.
The city abbreviates these hills
as they climb a few steps ahead of us
into the sky, the yellow
of winterkill laid bare by runoff.
Miles away the mountains spelled out
against the horizon have come to
rest like a jaw gone slack.
The rich air around us is sharp,
strands of barbed wire in the fences
parting easily, the wind too cold
for anyone to speak.
This kind of silence is solace,
joins us as we ease past
barbs that can snag like words in exposed skin.
Words we step between into the open.

Ecology

You were always and never the boy next door,
sat in the desk behind mine,
walked home with other friends, half a mile up,
the hills shaken out like ragged burlap
above Capri Avenue where you lived.
In high school, I loved you
with a passion I could not call love,

instead called ecology,
the 3 square feet of hillside we catalogued
under wind-torn sky, prairie
crocus and grasses, two types of sage,
red ants quick as blood, aphids nuzzling yellow
buffalo beans and pupa dreaming
among the roots, a world
to be sampled, an uncommon love.

We sat together, but apart
with other boys at lunch, played cards,
repeated the same jokes
about the girls in class.
I would look across the littered table
while you laughed; a faint
hint of beard flushed your cheek.

You found my letters after school
among your books, your gooseneck lamp
trained on paper unfolding
nomenclature you understood,
but never answered.
Instead you lent me your field notes,
sheet after sheet of precisely
drawn foothills plants.
I pored over them like pornography,
each life cycle labelled and explained.

You were always and never the boy next door.
Now we sleep with men in different cities,
collect them with an ardour not quite
expert, but studied nonetheless.
When a man lasts more than a few nights,
I might describe the secrets of that hillside
where nature touched us first,
describe how, over a lifetime, 3 square feet
of friendship become a country,
its soil wild and fruitful with desires
sampled, then elsewhere spent.

The Man from Grande Prairie

Already you have lived under my skin
longer than the one late hour when I held you in my arms.

You drew the curtains and we were in a room
of touch; my sightless fingers looked
for the way inside you, my hands like lanterns
shining down a forest road on a moonless night.
They amazed you.
Your breathing told me that my touch was light.

That night before I met you
my hands were cold.
I had walked through this cool
Ontario city to where I met you,
by chance, in a bar without a coat.
When at last we danced,
we danced under a cloak of coloured lights.

Your body in my arms warmed me
with its residue of clear Alberta air
that lingers on my hands.
Your sweat reeked of poplar wood and campfires,
of rounds sung about the flames
with laughter and an untuned guitar.
It reeked of the Rockies
overshadowing where I grew up.
I licked it off your skin,
your cock in my fist and in my mouth.

After we came, you told me
how you hate the northern town
where your mother bore you
and which you can't escape,
despise its pulp mill workers,
their hard hats and calloused ways.

You told me of the man in Calgary
who loved you then turned away.
For months you've lived out on RR 1
and told no one; in that remote
and lovely land you must be crazed.

My hands left heat on your skin
that you could not escape,
the surplus heat of remembered
cities, of garden homes
and unfolding suburban maps.
The next day, instead of meeting
as we arranged in a restaurant,
we met by chance on some corner
smouldering with rush hour traffic.
Not the parting you had wanted;
we shook hands, then you turned away.
Now, as you are flying homeward,
I will never get to ask.

We all carry a darkness inside us
that has nothing to do with
forest roads, cities, and moonless nights.
It is not what we are born to,
but it shadows forth within us
as we age, desire casting
silences longer than we can bear.
We all run before them, but must learn
to stop, learn to carry this darkness
toward each other with unblaming hands of light.

West Then East

In the city leaves are falling,
branches denuded by cold
gusts of rain pushing like a glacier down the Ottawa Valley,
In Andrew Haydon Park geese shelter
for the night among the dead
rushes grizzling the riverbanks.

Somewhere farther upriver it is still late summer.
You spread a blanket on fallow ground
your family cleared,
then gave up for town as the farm was failing.
We lie looking up through a circle
of ragged sky all afternoon,
blue with mosquitoes, sheltered from the sun
by the exposed walls of your grandmother's root cellar,
the earth floor choked with grass.
In a hundred years no one ever burned
it completely from the land.
When you were a boy, a thick-armed
cousin let you strike the match;
its flame scorched your fingers
as he undid your pants.
Our bodies join and I taste the smoke.
A fearful emptiness kindles deep
within as you massage
my chest, my stomach, my penis
hot and painful in your mouth,
a vacuum out of which tornadoes struggle,
touch down in Edmonton, tear shingles
like teeth from my sister's house.
Back in Ottawa, we hear about it hourly
on the news, the same black
funnel rising again and again above
and through those distant suburbs.

Still the weather taunts us, bears
down along the river,
our bodies bits of mismatched tectonic plate
chilled by the flat and angry land
I left behind; sudden
childhood winter storms cutting roads
across the prairies, towns pushed
far apart by blowing snow,
my family stranded Christmas Eve
at a White Rose station outside Lacombe.
After such winters how can I
be certain that I am warm?

Twilight and randomly the geese
descend, reflected
upward by the river, settling
into the cold liquid shades of dusk.
It is easy to call the flyway
above us freedom, though
sometimes while we talk — two men
who love each other,
who always talk — I listen for fading
valedictory cries
and the quiet before snowfall.

Acadia Notebook

Maine, 1992

I

Time geologic,
rising through the mist —

the scarred mountain lifts us
above a shore no one

is sure of through the haze
as we stumble

over rocks, along faults ripped
across upturned layer

upon layer of long settled
lake silt, finding our bearings

through heat condensing in our hair,
shaken down from white

pine needles and thinning
maples as the ocean

wind thuds in, last hurrah
of a far hurricane

awash against this
worn, inverted

bowl of a mountain which time
has turned

a gentle blind eye to,
after such appetite

for flood, for the collapsing
facades of remote cities,

which we left behind,
the idea of

at least, the exacting
maps folded neatly on the dash.

II

Fossils in the earth
loosed with great

passion, history read from the stilled
grains of pollen, the petrified

ash of infernal, prehistoric
fires, the bones

of nightmare fleshed
out by the granite

flanks we move over
through daylight, rising

into the mist a few steps
behind what we hope

is the present, a clearing
where we look down into the bottomless

fog of where we come from,
the bent branches and turning

leaves blazing
the trail like genes.

III

Crack open the thunder eggs,
collected like windfall

apples, the male and female
split apart but not

separable, the inside
of each weathered carapace

cradling the metamorphic
etiology of rock, the swirling

bloodstream of a brain cooled
to agate, the trace

elements of a long current
dailiness heavy in our veins.

IV

Who we are here
and where we come from:

no one will tell us,
though there is evidence —

fin patterns, on the journey
upward, of ancient fish

outlined in the sandstone record,
and, on an outcrop, graffiti

dated, enclosed in a primitive heart.
And finally,

the clearing we promised ourselves,
but not the view.

The violence of the earth
fogs us in

even as it dissipates,
our own passionate natures

no less cyclic,
conceived and passed down

the bloodline, storm by bloody storm,
this coast, these hearts used

to such ravages, hurricane-force.
Carbon-date what you can,

something inside us tells us,
isolate what cannot be

understood, for later generations,
in the showcases of the museum.

Each life leaves its shadowy remnant
of light on the soft clay

of time, every breath a living
history of the earth

inside,
outside our skins.

Lift

Spring again and the world
is glass, light fallen

overnight and frozen by sudden cold at dawn.
Branches reach up through thin

glittering windsocks that fragment
on the swell, tiny motes of light carried

in gusts across the almost
abandoned field of this airstrip where small

light planes take off through uncontrolled
airspace, morning melting in the heat

of the engines, heat spat
out by the glinting whir of propellers.

We stand below, sheltered
behind awkward terminal doors, inadequate

before each plane's mastery of lightness,
how each one navigates up through

the currents, buoyed on the thermals,
our eyes drawn after as one by one

the planes disappear into the north.
Something opens up over the wilderness,

discovers lakes;
why not our hearts?

Such emptiness aches for a sudden
lift upward, an overview

to map taiga softened by spring thaw.
Instead we hang back in the false

warmth of glass doors glazed with sun
while planes accelerate

down the runway and depart, having shed
last night's rain from their wings

in shards of ragged light, wreckage
we seldom make light of no matter how

much we want to,
no matter how hard we try.

Watch

You left your watch in my car;
I returned it, time lost

and recovered in your bed,
sex a seizure you seize me in,
your body a froth of sweat

given up to mine in fits
and starts.
                Time stops

momentarily, the crystal

shattered against the wall.
Hands quaver
in the throes of shock,

recover the slow pull
of minutes
and hours about an off-white face,
massage small
warm circles into the small

of my back, hands
that in the morning sometimes want

to set time back,

pull up zippers,
do up shirts, holes and exhausted
buttons not always

matching as I watch you dress.

Watches can be repaired more
easily than men.
Don't fall

in love with me, you said.

Answering Machine

Come in from the night.
Time is a voice

you might find waiting,
surprising
transcript of what I could not save,

face to face, for later,
                              words suspended
on coy
filaments of smoke,

voice upon time upon voice,

layers of anxious expectation recorded over
men who might have come before, love

flashing in the darkness.
Who is listening —
untimely

erasure of the hour anticipated even

as I speak and ever

present in each disembodied

fragment.

Timeless amnesia —
sometimes you won't even play the time
back once.

Sumac

Women are not the only ones
who bleed, a song

perhaps
            from some bygone era,
a mosquito-hum

of prairie where you then I
were born, men
as boys not at home

home on the awkward range of windy
blizzards or arid
flashes of summer heat

where cowboys ambushed us

behind rotting snow
fences in the park, anaesthetized

us with rapid
blanks in abandoned lots.

Here, time is gentle;

the red leaves fall like clockwork,

at their best before October 11th,
so someone said, the schedule

observed like the bloody
                              cycles of the moon,
sumac leaves, pieces
of time disintegrating in the back

alleys where we stop heedlessly

hand in hand,
each minute bleeding as it must in pools of rain.

You try to staunch this ecstatic
onslaught
                with clumsy kisses,
rain
drops hanging
                        from the scrubby
burdock of your unshaven
face.

Socks

Memory of waking

returning to our bodies
perhaps the last
morning, early light escaping

from the snows through

a gap in the blinds,
our bodies
chilled as we
disentangle from the worn

sheets and dress,
one final

glimpse of your back, the soft
hair matting the last
vertebrae of your spine.

Four identical socks
inside-out
on the floor, time reversed

and irreversible,
confused
in louvred shafts of light.

We each choose two,
not knowing

which are which, white

and nameless

hopes you might have had once,
indistinguishable

random as mine.

Stains

They are everywhere, accidental
and black on the sleeve
of my shirt, on the overstuffed arm
of the sofa in the lobby,
burned through the sheen
of the oak table we lean on
in silence, its pale plane
of light scored by some
careless eclipse, a cigarette
dropped after a meal of salmon,
white wine, and asparagus.
Green oxides bleed down the marble
facade of the hotel around us,
its copper mansard weeping,
weeping as it breaks down in the rain.

We carry the rain inside us,
carry it upstairs to bed, it courses
through us, soaked up by dreams
woven from blotting paper
once so unselfconscious and fresh,
now inked with shadows and retreating
faces we are slow to acknowledge,
waking to kicked off sheets
and saliva on the pillows.
Our bodies tangle, nerve ends
speculating on what the other
said in the night.

Wordless, flushed from love
and exhausted, I study the ceiling,
mildewed, liver-spotted
with drizzly afternoon light.
No longer able to lie
about permanence, whispering, whispering,
I ease away while you doze,
the print that my spine urged
into your stomach
still pink, but fading.

Outside, beyond the terrace,
the ocean's constant erasure.
Gone are the sunlit days
when we unrolled towels on the sand.
Light stained everything;
we darkened, magnified
by the delicious lens of the sun.
We were insatiable.
We ate clams, drank beer,
and for a while saw what we chose,
saw our faces emblazoned on the surface
of tidal pools, not in the milky
spawning of hermit crabs
among the starfish below.

Meech Lake, Late Afternoon

The lake blues deeply,
clouds piling up after a day of heat,

the water clear as rain.
I look back as we swim farther out,

away from the windy green
reflections of trees nudging

from shore, your head above water,
waves tipping over us as we rise

for air above stones sunk below
eyesight, far apart as stars

whose light like oxygen
has yet to dissolve, open

in rings through the cool
retina at the back of the sky,

light we are told spreads
towards us through this sheer

blue curtain of daylight;
which we pull wide

at night, hoping or not hoping,
the sky as it is

always bright, always enough.
We swim still farther.

Our limbs glow from effort
as the lake opens, closes about us,

resumes its profound and sun-waved
demeanour, our bodies momentary

breaths of light more and less
of the moment as we kick

from the narrows, the voices
on shore not calling

for us, but fading.
This is what we came for:

not the turning back, which we will give
into sooner than later,

but the absence ahead,
where we hang

clouds above, weeds below,
secret and at last approachable.

Continuity

At present, this is the last poem.
This is the only poem
I have been waiting for, or so it now appears.
It approaches me in the late evening

dining room of an old lover who walks in and out of the present
from the kitchen where he is making
soup as he always has since before we met,
cucumbers from his garden blended
with savory he grew from seed and picked himself, the genesis

of a premonition sown last spring, an image
even then of himself standing
at the window looking down on today's wind-ragged peonies,
the harvested, weightless rows of peas and runner beans
while the pot idles on the red-hot element, sunset
condensing against the tense
mirror of the horizon,
the house empty, and I am already gone, long gone, *disparu*.

But this poem is not about him.
Somewhere in the more recent past I have just met you.
Your words alter me reminiscently over a meal.

Last night you told me that you could never love
me the way he tried to, the dark
September sky overshadowing us with the scarred, hungry
fullness of your eyes and the moon.
No longer will you believe love
between two men can ever last.

This is not what I imagine,
imagined how you might want our lives
to join with days and nights we would look back on,
drives in the wilderness and arguments
under the same roof, trailing
ivy and exchanged books, Easter
with your family, Thanksgiving with mine, plans
for winter holidays south on the Gulf Coast.

Still, at 2 A.M. when I left, you
gave me a hug, tired
hands tentatively rubbing my shoulders.
This is what I give back, the last
and only poem
at present and the first about friendship.

Road, River, Snake

The river is frozen, though
in places, glimpsed from the road

slow warmth radiates upwards,
ragged openings in the ice

where something never healed over.
It sleeps under the surface

there for the duration,
some luxuriant snake hibernating.

An endless belly melts through
in torn patches of gray-green

muscle caught by the sun.
My car hugs its curves,

rises, falls, tips
toward the river from each

vantage above this cold
and sky-blue country I now call home.

I achieve another turn.
It burns inside me, such a sudden

unnarrowing of the river
where toppled expanses of cracking ice

vent long held breaths, white and steamier than Vesuvius.
Yet it is so still,

not one incautious white-tailed deer picks
its way across this changing waste,

not one breeze shakes the maples
free of wanting any comforting camouflage of leaves.

The whole of it exposes me bit
by bit, each day as I drive this

way to work, my hands and feet shifting
the car into much higher speeds.

My heart shifting.
Sluggish serpents of blood at last

heat my body; the river, thawing, uncoils
by osmosis toward the ocean

through my very cells.

California Notebook

I

In Monterey County, a father and son
rest shirtless in the afternoon heat.
Cloud cover breaks over a field of artichokes
as they crouch at the centre
of it all, at the edge of the Pacific,
among the neatly tilled rows,
passing a thermos of iced tea between them,
yellow hills and the farm buildings in the distance
peeling a genealogy of layered
white paint into the drought-sickened soil

while in San Francisco, on Castro Street,
the family tree has come to an end.
Men meet for brunch;
they meet to play tennis, meet
for the first time in bed
on the second floor of a Victorian rowhouse
that has been lovingly restored.
Lace in the bay window bellies to the wind
while they drowse, the sheets caught about them
weightless as the banks
of fog that tear, founder against Twin Peaks.

In this city, the whole of nature
is never far, the bay
glimpsed downhill
from a cable car as it climbs into Chinatown,
Alcatraz rising into view on its pedestal of rock,
a city ripped along racial lines like any other,
black bars along Fillmore
and the HIV+ homeless scavenging
for handouts among the flower stalls at Union Square;
wave upon wave of men released from the subway
at Church Street, men with well cropped hair
on the way home to a lover or a book,
local wine under their toned arms;
and other men with women who step from
the tram for several stops later
along Golden Gate Park, salt spray
and eucalyptus coating their skin,
to be licked off later
after dinner, after mowing the lawn,
every neighbourhood shaken by the periodic
passions of the San Andreas fault,
the whole Bay Area spellbound
watching Oakland burn, black smoke
boiling up over the hills as the fire
overruns house after house,
commuters lying face down on the freeway,
letting it pass over them while
redwoods, flush with embers,
shake them off like a dog out of water
and, unlike the rest of us,
 simply go on.

II

Carlos, I hardly knew you
and simply can't
go on, the spring of your touch

meeting mine, electric as a storm
in March pushing over the city,
the lights of the Phoenix
dim, wavering over the dance floor as you
led me into the centre,
a fragmented geography of dance outlined
in the strobe-lit movements about us.

Carlos, I hardly knew you,
but you took me
out into the night, a brief tremor
of wind along Castro Street as we talked,

hand in hand past stores and restaurants closed hours before,
past other men settled on benches
in couples, by beds of agapanthus and jasmine.

We stopped under a madrone tree
and told stories,

parted without a kiss,
you to the dance floor and me to my hotel,
first a street corner, then a taxi ride and fog,
the bond between us one of respect,

the separateness of our lives acknowledged,
our bodies neighbouring countries
not to be overrun
by random passions that might leave scars —

Carlos, I hardly knew you,
your skin sheltered by exquisite layers of denim and cotton,
your voice, your stories, your questions,

your eyes dark as Guatemalan coffee —

I carry it all with me,
a token, a keepsake, a tiny triangle
of hope, a tongue print

we might have left on each other
and indelibly
trusted, reinventing the family
like many lovers before us

if we had more time.

III

What a continent —
San Francisco to Toronto,

a link scored by the jetstream,
flying above the interior of a continent,

above what to some is pure
barrenland herringboned with roads,

our interior lives a relay of misconnections
thrown by satellite into deepest space,

our most private aspirations
broadcast on the expiring network of stars,

tapped into and decoded by the radio telescopes
focused on Andromeda at Mt. Palomar.

The astronomers hardly know us,
but outside the 767's window —

San Francisco rises out of the fog
that overtakes it,

the Sacramento River struggles through
its mouth to San Pablo Bay expanding,

contracting like a lung, the current mixing
with salt water, an afterthought of breath —

the resuscitating kiss of life, if we are careful;
the improprieties we sometimes release

into the lifeforce of the river show nothing but
indifference, indifference and death.

As an airplane banks overhead,
a whole continent of men looking westward.

Learning how to be safe, learning
not to give way.

The Nevada mountains pushing
into glaciers, into the unforgettable cold

fact of their own existence and upheaval.
Discovering the Utah lakes,

shorelines etched
with tantalizing discharges of salt,

the geophysics of the erotic,
of where we were born

making less difference now,
men lying together with a decade

less fear in the cornfields outside Des Moines,
lying in the open on condominium

balconies in Minneapolis and Detroit,
dusk flaring

veins of carmine above our daily lives
of shopping, politics, and work.

As this plane flies eastward
bringing to Canada Customs its cargo of dreams.

Acknowledgements

I would like to thank the following journals where some of these poems originally appeared, sometimes in slightly different forms:

Canada: *The Canadian Forum, Canadian Literature, Dandelion, The Fiddlehead, Grain, Lubricité, The Malahat Review, Matrix, NeWest Review, Poetry Canada Review, Prairie Fire, Quarry, Queen's Quarterly, TickleAce, The University of Windsor Review.*

United States: *Backspace, The Chiron Review, Christopher Street, The Evergreen Chronicles, The James White Review.*

"Mnemonics" first appeared in *Capital Poets: An Ottawa Anthology*, Colin Morton, ed. (Ouroboros, 1989); "Indian Graveyard, Gulf of Georgia, 1968" in *More Garden Varieties* (League of Canadian Poets/Mercury Press, 1989); "Lift," in honour of Robin Skelton, in *Something More Than Words* (Reference West, 1991). "Who is this" in *Symbiosis*, Luciano Diaz, ed. (Girol Books, 1992); and "Best Man" in *Reconcilable Differences*, Christopher Levenson, ed. (Bayeux, 1994). "Physcial," "Ecology," "Indian Grave Yard, Gulf of Georgia, 1968," and "Parallel Lanes" were collected in *physical* (Midfire Press, 1993).

Quotes are drawn from "Natural Theology," by Robert Hass, in *Human Wishes* (Ecco, 1989); *An American Childhood*, by Annie Dillard (Harper & Row, 1987); *The Body and Its Dangers,* by Alan Barnett (St. Martin's, 1990); "Skunk Hour," by Robert Lowell, in *Life Studies* (Farrar, Straus, and Cudahy, 1959); and "This Sullen Art," by Anne Szumigalski, in *Doctrine of Signatures* (Fifth House, 1983).

Writing is a solitary art, thank God, but praise be to those who listen, criticize, and appreciate. I would like to thank the community of writers in Ottawa, who were first to hear many of these poems. In particular, thanks go to Blaine Marchand, Nadine McInnis, and Sandra Nicholls. Thanks also to Anne Szumigalski, whose editorial advice was a pleasure to consider.

"City in the Foothills" is dedicated to Patricia Young; "Delivery" to my brother-in-law, Dave Schroder; "Stickmen" to Carl McMurray; "Best Man" to Stephen Borrow and Bonnie Kelly; "For Magie at the Bedside of Her Dying Friend" to Magie L. Dominic; "The Aqua-Nuns" to Rita Donovan; "Vernix" to Elizabeth-Anne Malischewski; "Ecology" to Doug Torrance; "Lift" and "Road, River, Snake" to Nadine McInnis, "California Notebook" to James Gurley and Jennifer Vine, "Acadia Notebook" and "Meech Lake, Late Afternoon" to Philip Robert. "Patriarchy" is written in memory of Patricia Allen.